AF472218

Young Girl's Poetry

Books One, Two and Three

SECOND EDITION

Acknowledgements

Aunt Jean, Uncle Larry, Tangi, Koko, Nate, Nailah, Kinaya, and everyone in my family.

Mrs. Shepard (I love you too!)

My BFF, SANDY!! (love u^_^)

All my friends and teachers (especially MRS. WRIGHT. YOU ROCK!!)

And of course the graduating Class of '06 at SCL!!!

I love you all. Thank you so much for believing in me. You all have helped me grow so much. In my writing and in life. Without any of you, I wouldn't have gotten this far.

P.S. – If I did not note your name, I apologize. But just know you are in my thoughts and heart. Whoever was not mentioned personally, you are still noted. Either as family or friends. Many thanks for all the support! Love you!!

Dedication...

I would like to dedicate this book to my best friend, Sandy. And of course my graduating class from SCL (St. Catherine Laboure):

The

CLASS OF '06 and '10!!!

I love you all!

Aaron Alan* Alexis* Alissa* Amber* Ana* Andy* Anthony A* Anthony M* Autumn* Ben* Brian* Caitlyn* Carla* Christina G* Daniel* Danny* David G* David H* Faye* Ian* Jamela* Jane* Janell* Janet* Jason* Jenell* Jerry* Joanne* Joey* John* Jon* Joseph* Kristina* Kristine* Luis* Marian* Matthew* Maya* Melissa* Michael* Molly* Natalia* Patrick* Paul* Priscilla* Rebecca* Reina* Richard* Sachi* Samuel* Sandra* Sarah* Shelbi* Tierney* Aaron* Alan* Alexis* Alissa* Amber* Ana* Andy* Anthony A* Anthony M* Autumn* Ben* Brian* Caitlyn* Carla* Christina G* Daniel* Danny* David G* David H* Faye* Ian* Jamela* Jane* Janell* Janet* Jason* Jenell* Jerry* Joanne* Joey* John* Jon* Joseph* Kristina* Kristine* Luis* Marian* Matthew* Maya* Melissa* Michael* Molly* Natalia* Patrick* Paul* Priscilla* Rebecca* Reina* Richard* Sachi* Samuel* Sandra* Sarah* Shelbi* Tierney* Aaron* Alan* Alexis* Alissa* Amber* Ana* Andy* Anthony A* Anthony M* Autumn* Ben* Brian* Caitlyn* Carla* Christina G* Daniel* Danny* David G* David H* Faye* Ian* Jamela* Jane* Janell* Janet* Jason* Jenell* Jerry* Joanne* Joey* John* Jon* Joseph* Kristina* Kristine* Luis* Marian* Matthew* Maya* Melissa* Michael* Molly* Natalia* Patrick* Paul* Priscilla* Rebecca* Reina* Richard* Sachi* Samuel* Sandra* Sarah* Shelbi* Tierney* Aaron* Alan* Alexis* Alissa* Amber* Ana* Andy* Anthony A* Anthony M* Autumn* Ben* Brian* Caitlyn* Carla* Christina G* Daniel* Danny* David G* David H* Faye* Ian* Jamela* Jane* Janell* Janet* Jason* Jenell* Jerry* Joanne* Joey* John* Jon* Joseph* Kristina* Kristine* Luis* Marian* Matthew* Maya* Melissa* Michael* Molly* Natalia* Patrick* Paul* Priscilla* Rebecca* Reina*

Class of '06 @SCL!!!

Coming Soon.......

also by Tierney Oshae'

A Child's Heart: A Young Girl's Story

and more poetry

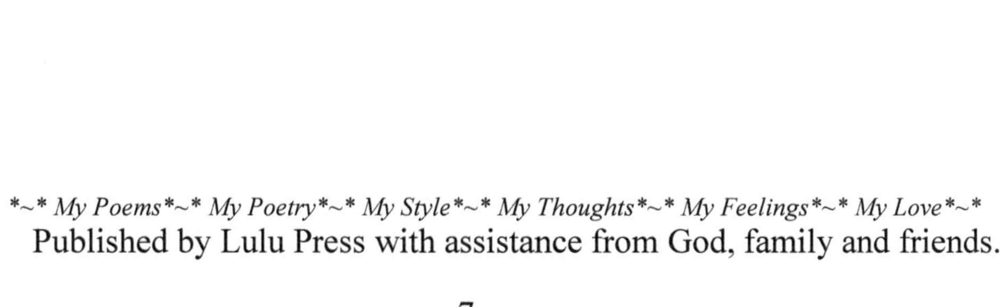

Published by Lulu Press with assistance from God, family and friends.

Young Girl's Poetry

Books One, Two and Three

By

Tierney Oshae'

Contents

Book One: My Poems

Book Two: My Poetry

Book Three: My Heart

BOOK ONE:

~My Poems~

Poems 1-8

Poem #1: *Unity and Love (A prayer to God)*

Oh dear God,
What is Unity?
What is Love?
Unity and Love,
Will it keep us all together?
Can fulfilled destiny out last all that is wrong or evil?
Oh Lord, please Show and Give us your love,
Give us your knowledge...in all,
In so many different ways.
With you in our life God,
I believe we can fulfill our destiny.
And it will out last all evil.
We will be kept together,
United we will stand.
We shall have the ability to see clearly.
See clearly through each other's eyes.
We will gain a greater insight on one another's life.
But only this can happen if we are allowed your

knowledge,
Your great knowledge and love,
True love for everything.
All I can say is thank you.
Thank you, God.
Thanks for everything.

Amen.

Poem #2 : ***Lost (Darkness)***

Lost,
With no way out.
Darkness,
A black, scary darkness appears.
Slowly it gets closer toward me.
Soon it reaches me.
Help me!
Oh someone please help me!
For I don't like the darkness.
This great scary darkness.
Darkness can take me away.
It will take me away.
Away.
Oh so far away.
Away from my home, my beautiful home.
My family, my loved ones, my heart.
My home and the light.
The bright beautiful light.
Light of day.

First say prayers and good-byes,
After, the light will go.
Then a cold gust of wind will come.
But only when the messenger has come.
The mist.
The mist, both scary and dark, shall take
me.
It shall take my heart.
Sweetness has disappeared,
Leaving a soul empty.
A soul empty and no longer pure.
Cold blood and a stone cold heart will
remain,
And a cold, empty soul will also remain.
Only one sane imagine the pain,
The sadness.
Sorrow surrounding one's only escape
Only exit, getaway.
An escape way back home.
A getaway back to pureness.
An exit back to sweetness and light.
Oh so pure and kind, the light was.

Now it is gone.
The beauty on light,
Gone. Forever.
Now replaced,
Replaced by an empty place.
A melancholy place.
No more happiness,
No joy.
But that's what darkness can and will do,
If you're alone. All alone,
Oh so alone,
Even with only sadness as your only friend.
You're still alone.

Poem #3: Flowers

What do you think?
About these things that smell oh so sweet.
They wave in the blowing wind,
Back and forth.
They wave along to the beat.
The beat of their own beautiful music.
A beat only they can hear,
But another can hear also.
One who understands their true beauty.
They are beautiful and oh so lovely.
Together they stand,
Not one lonely.
Not one out of place or order.
But once they fall, they are divided.
Out of place.
Listen to my words closely.
Though they will be divided,
You should pick one.
Pick one everyday.

Cause no matter what happens,
Their beauty will bring you joy.
Happiness will fill your soul.
Just like us they are special,
They are different.
Unique in every single way.
So remember,
Pick one.
No matter what size it is,
Or condition it is in.
Bring out their joyfulness through you.

Poem #4: *The Rose (Meaning)*

Oh my, what beauty,
What dazzle and flare.
Red, a pure red.
A bloody red.
Deep, lovely blood red.
And yet, it is a mere flower.
As small, quiet, and timid as a flower can be.
A red rose to be exact,
The smallest rose here in the garden.
A true la rosa chica I say.
What is a "Rose"?
Radiant, open, sensitive, elegant?
This is its meaning to me.
But I wonder,
Wonder if I am rose.
Am I a rose?
Am I truly radiant, open, sensitive, and elegant?
Somehow, I believe I am.

How about you?

Are a rose?

Radiant, open, sensitive, and elegant?

I think so.

If you believe this, everyone will.

To me, we are all roses.

At least at one point in our life.

What do you really think?

Poem #5: *Lost Little Girl*

Fear, sadness,
That is what I see.
I see it all in her eyes.
They are empty and filled with sorrow.
Is she lost?
That's how it appears to be.
She is lost.
Lost in a deserted place.
But wait, it's more than just a place.
It is a room.
A room with only one bed and pillows.
Pillows scattered across the floor.
It is empty,
Empty just like her eyes.
Her small, innocent eyes.
She is abandoned and alone.
All alone.
Without a real home.
A home is truly more than a house or a place
of residence.

It is a place where you feel safe, and loved.
Inside and out.
Without that, she is homeless.
Homeless inside.
No parents, no love.
So I'll comfort her.
Give her hugs and make her feel loved.
For she is sorrowing.
Calling out for love.
For a true home in all our hearts.

Poem # 6: Prayer for Me

I see a little boy,
Praying softly and quietly.
Only God knows what he is praying for.
What or whom is he praying for?
Is he praying for selfish things or for loved ones?
Or is he praying for me?
Me and others in the world.
We all need a prayer,
But is he praying for us?
We who are in despair or pain,
We who may have sinned one too many times,
We who have lost the ones we loved with all our heart,
Or for the families of those who have died in the war.
This may never be answered.
Unless I ask him.
Or ask God.

For now I will just sit here wondering.
Wondering if another is praying for me.
Until I meet with God and ask who has prayed for me,
I'll wonder.
Wonder and pray.
I'll say a prayer for others.
Others who have less than I do,
And for others with more than I.
I will also say a prayer for the boy I see.
Pray that he is ok too.
That he is loved and safe.
For we all need prayers.
No matter what size they are.

Poem # 7: A Child's Tears

Tears.
Tears from a little girl.
She seems to be crying.
Who is she holding onto?
Who is trying to comfort her?
Is that her mother or a friend?
Or is it a woman who just shows she cares?
I don't know.
But why is the girl crying?
She is wearing a princess's tiara,
A tiara that shines in the light.
Almost every girl wants to wear one,
Become a princess and rule over her royal court.
Has the princess been told to put her toys away?
Or did the queen get mad at her majesty?
I pause and think.
Maybe she has lost the queen or king.
Or have they left her and gone to the kingdom in the sky?

A sweet way of saying they have passed on.
I'll go comfort her and make her smile.
Tell her things will be fine.
Even just a quick smile will do for me.
Just a smirk will make me feel as if things are ok.
I'll pray for her, day and night
Pray that she will recover from her sadness and sorrow.

Poem #8: An 8th Grader's Farewell

The time has come at last.
A time for us to depart from each other.
Move on and fulfill our academic dreams.
But only for some time we will be together.
A summer or maybe just a few weeks.
Nevertheless,
I know we all will meet again.
Whether it's in five years, or even ten.
Whether it's a school reunion,
Or just on the street.
I guess that it's true what they say,
"You never realize how much something means to you,
Until you lose it."
Sad to say,
I didn't realize how good we had it.
All of us together.
We had tons of bumps in the road,
Yet we still kept going.
Strive for what we felt was right.
From new teachers to bad grades.

We've been through almost everything.
Not to mention we have all either struggled,
And achieved in different aspects.
Both have been a great challenge.
But hey,
We made it through.
Together.
I can never forget those moments,
Good and bad.
Happy and sad.
I would say our bond is more than a friendship,
It's a family.
A weird, awkward, yet loving family.
We fuss and fight together,
Blaming one another for something.
We got into trouble with the principal and vice,
Plus teachers and other members of faculty.
Though we did not enjoy this one bit,

We stuck it out.
And now,
It's over.
All our old memories from this school are over.
Now our new memories begin.
"When one door closes, another opens"
That quote is so true.
Though we are leaving each other,
We will still be with one another,
In both our minds and hearts.
Remember me and I'll remember you.
Forever.
Names may be forgotten,
But the events we shared will be remembered.
And we'll tell them to our children.
Hopefully we'll meet up again.
Meet up and share our memories.
Memories and special moments.
Good-bye friends and foes.
Until we meet up again,
This is my farewell.
My 8th grade farewell.

Book Two:

~*My Poetry*~

Poems #9 -16

Poem #9: Love

Love,
A controversial thing.
Something everyone wants,
And something everyone hates.
It can heal, it can hurt.
Love,
Dangerous, Harmless.
Beautiful, Ugly.
Easy, Hard.
Soft, Tough.
No matter the type of love,
Everyone gives or has it.
They are not always known,
But the love of God.
The love He has for you,
For us.
That my friends,
That is known.
In our hearts and our souls.

Poem #10: Tears

Here we go again.

Ups and downs,

Ins and outs.

Laughing and smiling one minute,

Then crying and yelling the next.

And then, tears.

When it's all over,

There are only tears.

Sobbing in silence,

Sobbing into a pillow.

A white pillow,

So soft and warm.

But it soon turns cold,

Oh so very cold.

Coldness from those tears,

Tears, which have fallen from my cheek.

Warm yet cold,

Salty and wet.

Yet the tears still fall.

And this must stop,

This crying thing.

No more tears,

No more pain.

No more waiting up late by my window pain.

Day and night,

Waiting for you.

I will miss you though,

My love, my heart.

Now I say farewell,

Leaving you with hugs and kisses.

Good-bye my love,

My daddy dearest.

Poem #11: Family

What is a family?
A mom and a dad,
A brother and a sister?
Cousins, aunts, and uncles?
Or is it a group of people who care?
Care for you and your well-being.
Is a gang family?
Or an exclusive clique?
This quest for the true meaning may never be answered,
By man at least.
As for me,
A family can be whatever you want,
As long as it involves God's love in the relation.
The relation of family.
If everything stated is true,
Then I have a huge family.
All different and all mine.
I guess when you think of it,
We're all family.

Through God’s eyes and in our souls.
His love and the love for one another,
It unites us together.
All together.
One big family,
God’s Family.

Poem #12: A Message from An Angel (original)

Little girl,

Listen to what I have to say.

Your mother has gone,

And your daddy has to go away.

Far away.

He says good-bye,

Sending hugs and kisses.

Bundles of love.

I've come from heaven, my child.

From my loving and quiet home,

Heaven.

But because I love you so,

And care for your well-being...

I've come to guard.

Guard and protect you from evil.

Until that very day your sickness takes you away.

Away from this horrid land,

Into the skies.

When this time comes,

Though it will be soon,

I will come and take you by your hand.

Your soft, little hand.

I shall lead you to the gates.

Those big, white gold, pearly gates,

With a luxurious glow surrounding it.

A man will be in the front of the gate,

Awaiting your arrival.

He will be in a chair at a desk.

He shall ask you your name and if you've been good.

Tell the truth, only the truth.

For liars don't go to heaven,

They go below the earth.

Hell,

The liars' home.

But not to worry,

Things will go fine.

When he lets you in,

You will go to a playroom filled with kids.

Babies, Toddlers, Teens, and ALL in between.

There you will see Lily Ann.

Lily Ann Turner,

Your baby sister.

Then you'll see April,

Little April, your cousin.

Last, you shall see Katherine,

Katherine Turner, your mother.

Why are they here, you say?

Well, remember the accident,

They were in it.

Now they're here,

Safe and sound.

Go and hug them.

Hug them tight,

Don't let go.

Your daddy will not be there.

At least for a while.

If he is good, he can come with you.

But until the time comes,

Be good.

Listen to your Granny and Grandpa.

Kiss and hug them, too.

Love them, as I love you.

Until we meet again, I say good-bye.

Good-Bye, Sweetie.

Be good and I will take you up.

Up to stay with me.

Love will guard and guide you,

Until we met up again.

Poem #13: Message from an Angel (Remake)

Children,
Listen to what I say.
Teachers will be gone soon,
And friends will go away.
They will say good-bye,
Sending hugs and kisses.
Bundles of love.
I came down from heaven, my children,
Because I love you so.
To tell you a message,
A message from the Father.
He wants me to guard you all,
Keep you safe.
And let you know you're loved.
A greater love than your friends can give.
Though you are leaving them,
It is ok.
Your love for them will still live,
Live in you and in them.
Forever I will stay with you,
My love will guard and guide you.
Forever and ever.
Until the end of time.

Poem #14: Secret Valentines

It's Valentine's Day,
Everyone is having fun.
Gifts being given,
Love being spread.
But to tell you the truth,
It's all in your head,
Or maybe in your heart.
To me it's both.
The head and heart I mean.
It's funny,
This day we celebrate.
People give you cards,
People give you presents.
Given chocolates and roses,
Teddy bears and LOVE notes.
That's only some gifts,
Gifts for teens and kids.
The adults get the party,
The fun.
To them it is all fun.
But what about loners?

Those who are lonely.
Lonely with no one to love them.
I'm lonely,
Lonely in a sense of not having a lover.
So I am asking you now,
And only this time:
Can you love tender?
Can you be my Secret Valentine?
No one shall know,
I swear I won't tell.
Just wanna have someone,
Someone to care.
You don't have to love me,
Not one bit.
But you will have to be there,
There when I need love.
There when I need care.
I'll love you anyway,
No matter where you are.
Man I sprung,
On Cloud Nine.
Won't you please,
Please be mine?
My own Secret Valentine.

Poem #15: Pain and Sadness

Pain and Sadness.
The unpleasant, internal version of ying & yang,
Or the tormented couple known as Romeo &Juliet.
Everyone feels their presence,
Some more than others…like me.
It is a pair I feel enters me silently,
Oh so often.
Danger nears,
More pain enters.
Darkness without light,
More sadness comes.
Soulfulness is gone.
Good-Bye happiness and love,
And hello pain and sadness.
Welcome, I say.
I want you to go but I want you to stay.
Come in for a while,
But not for long.
A short while.
For everyone needs company.

Poem #16: Secret Love for You

Can you love someone?
Someone different from you.
One who looks or acts the opposite,
One with a distinct characteristics.
Will you love that person?
Love them with unconditional love.
I will.
No matter how you look,
No matter how you act.
Whether we part or remain together,
My love will be with you.
I would shout it out to the world:
"I LOVE U!"
But only if I could.
I can't though,
For your reputation is at stake.
Amazing how little things make people dislike you.
A little thing like "hello" or "how are you".
Even "I love you".
So because I love you,
I will keep this to myself.

But first I want to let you know,
Let you know how I feel.
Only you and I will know,
It will be our own secret.
No one will know,
This I promise.

BOOK THREE:

My Heart

Poems # 17 - 24

Poem # 17: Key to My Heart

My love is simple,
It has no price.
All you have to know is one thing:
Treat me right.
Respect me and I'll respect you.
Love me and I'll love you.
I'll give you more,
More of everything.
More love,
More care.
I'll give you it all,
Support and Trust.
But hey,
All you need to give is one thing:
The ability to treat me right.
That's the Key.
The Key to my heart.
Love and compassion,
We'll never be apart.
Say "I Love U",
But you gotta mean it.
Mean every word.
I'll say "I Love U",
Know that it is true.
Just love me,
Like I love you.
You are mine,
And wanna know a secret:
Wanna know the true Key?
Love.
True and tender.
Your love only.
Love is all I need.
True Love,
That's the Key.
The Golden Key.
Key to My Heart.

Poem # 18: Letting Go

It's hard to let go.
Let go of all the pain,
All of the sadness.
All those bitter-sweet memories,
Memories of you and me.
We had some bad times,
Just like everyone does.
It was weird for us though,
For it was you who I thought I could trust.
Trust you to be loyal,
Loving and true.
To me and only I.
But I guess it was a lie.
A lie that I felt would never become true,
At least from you.
My love, my heart,
My pal most caring.
I have to let go,
I have to come clean.
Let you go,
Say goodbye.
No longer needing you,
You and your love.
Goodbye, my love.
Goodbye for good,
Forever.
Time to let go,
Let go of you.
Forever.

Poem # 19: What's Love?

What's Love?
Some call it a feeling,
A tricky emotion.
Devious at the most.
Hidden in many disguises.
Disguises that are hidden beneath other emotions.
Anger,
Being mean to one another.
Pulling hair,
Tripping each other.
But in reality,
They really care.
Love.
A mystery,
One that cannot be solved.
They say they've found love,
And you ask how they know.
Some say: It's just a feeling you get.
They say it when someone makes you feel good,
Feel happy and special.
So now we know,
At least from one's perspective.
But not all.
So I'll just wonder,
Wonder for a while.
At least until that time.
That time when I fall,
Fall in love.
Whatever it is.

Poem # 20: If I Die Today…(Set Free)

If I die today,
Tell my mother I love her.
And my father I'd miss him,
Even though that would be a lie.
We had never met,
So what would be the point.
I'd tell my aunt I love her, too.
More than anyone I ever knew.
But then there is my uncle,
I love him too.
So if you can,
Please do this for me:
Tell everyone that I care,
But only for those who care about me.
During my last breaths I take,
My last moments here,
Just want you to know this:
I love you.
Watch over my family,
I'll watch over you.
Tell everyone I'll miss them,
Love them forever.
Tell them I'll be okay.
This is His plan,
His plan for me.
And one thing I know,
This plan is a good thing.
Wanna know the plan?
It's to be free.
To be who I wanna be,
Worry-free.
I wanna be free,
And now is my time.
My soul has been *Set Free*.

Poem # 21: Message to God

How do you send a message to God?
How do you let Him know what you wish to tell?
Do you mail it to Him,
To Heaven: Blessed Blvd. in Spiritual, Heaven 10910
Can you email it to him?
Email it to: www.heaven.org/G_O_D/
His email address is 000_GODS_LOVE@heaven.org
I guess,
I don't really know.
But you know,
I've seemed to have found a way.
Prayer.
It may seem as if it does not work,
But trust.
It does,
Try it some time.
It works and has a great affect.
Just believe,
Believe with all your heart.
He can help you,
Help you through all your troubles.
He'll do this for one reason.
He loves you.
Show him your love,
Pray to Him.
Send an IM mentally.

Poem # 22: Death and Life

Death,
Something that happens naturally.
Everyone dies,
Leaves this miserable yet pleasant place.
But can you die and still live?
Can you live through death?
I know the answer,
It's yes.
Yes you can die and still live.
Wanna know how?
You don't have to die physically,
You can die emotionally.
Spiritually and mentally.
When you love someone and lose them,
They still live.
Live in your heart and soul.
That's only when death is physical.
Mentally they are still here,
When they die.
But because I have died,
Emotionally, I mean.
Losing a loved one can screw you over, mess you up.
In away that's death,
Death mentally and emotionally.
Physically you're still there.
Living life,
Learning to love it.
But can you love it?
Can you love life?
That I can't answer,
For I have died and still lived.
But I have not loved life,
Not fully at least.
Learn to love life,
Can it help you live?
Or can it just hurt?
I don't know,

You answer that.
But do you think I am right?
You can die yet still live?
I say yes,
But what do you say?
Can you face DEATH and still LIVE?

Poem # 23: All I Need

I'm gonna let you know this,
This one little thing.
You may not believe me,
Or you may just disagree.
The truth is,
You're all I need.
No matter the time,
No matter the place,
You're always there for me.
Right there,
By my side.
Through thick and thin,
Fighting to help me win.
Win my courage,
My fulfillment.
I don't need anyone else but you.
I dont need money or gifts,
Jewels of all kinds.
All I need is love,
Someone to trust.
I never will let you go,
Leave you behind.
I know you'll do the same,
We are alike in ways.
But in others we're one-of-a kind.
Two peas in a pod,
I guess you can say.
To tell the truth,
I wanna keep it that way.
But when we part,
Know one other thing:
We are always together,
Connected at heart.
Never forget me,
I'll never forget you.
Because you're my strength,
You're all I need.

Poem #24: Wanted

Ever felt empty,
Empty inside.
Like something's missing.
Or like you want someone to need you,
Need you like you need them.
I do.
I know this feeling,
I have it come to me often.
A feeling to be needed.
The need to be wanted.
Wanted by someone,
One who cares.
Don't leave me,
That's all I can say.
When you're wanted,
There is no need to say this.
It's already there.
I want to feel WANTED,
WANTED by everyone.
Even you.

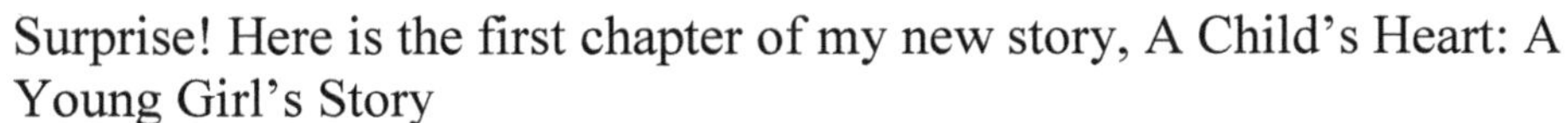

Sneek Peak!

Surprise! Here is the first chapter of my new story, A Child's Heart: A Young Girl's Story

(Look for it to come out soon.)_Enjoy this little snippet!

Tierney Oshae`

A Child's Heart: a young girl's story

Narrated By: Trinity Bernadette

If I had a diary, with a lock and a key, that held my secrets… all my sorrows and pains, I'd hold it tight and never let it out my sight. I know many people think I have a great life and lots of love. That may be true to most, but as for me… my life could be better. Yes it is true that I have tons of family and friends who love me, but I still want more. I keep holding on to my dreams like everyone, famous or not, says for kids to do.

Sadly and slowly my dream may be going away from me. I know it's hard to believe that a thirteen year old girl going on fourteen, who has dreams and aspirations of being a huge movie star, can easily say she is loosing her dream. Well let me tell you this now, for me it is hard to hold on to something I love so much. That love is acting and performing in front of others. I have taken many classes for this particular area of the performing arts and have been told I am exceptionally good. I believe everyone who tells me I'm gonna be famous but there is a minor problem, and with that there is an even larger problem.

The minor problem is that I am shy. But hey, when I get on stage and see all those faces in the audience, of course I get nervous, yet something comes over me and tells me I gonna do just fine and that's how I shine. Now that we have figured out that minor difficulty, here is the larger problem: Auditions! You see I am not rich, not what so ever, but my family has enough to survive and that's what really matters. Any way, auditions are my larger problems in reaching my dream. Here are three reasons why: first of all they usually cost money, secondly I am kinda nervous on whether they'll like me or not, and thirdly I need transportation. I search the net almost all the time looking for auditions, and after 4 months I found out that it's very difficult to find child/teenage auditions and be able to fit all of the features of the character you wish to apply for.

Trust, with my talent I can play almost any emotion or style (dramatic/comedy) you throw at me. My family and friends love my comedic skills because I can put a smile on their face when they are sad, depressed, or happy. Ask any of them and most will say I got talent. That's what I love to hear from someone. Whether they are friends, family, or just someone I associate with. Talent: Everyone has it and uses it in different ways. This is something that makes me different from others. Uniqueness, something I keep with me constantly. Maybe it is because of my family and friends support. Maybe it's the drive, the passion, the desire I've got for what I love but am slowly losing. Oh yeah, I forgot to tell you. My name is Trinity Bernadette. In this very story, you'll be able to understand me a bit better.

Want more? Then be on the look out for my next book, A Child's Heart: a young girl's story. The story is told through a young girl's point of view but has some facts from a true story.

Available for purchase

at Lulupress.com

The Love Jesus Showed
Can Never Be...
Compared!
His death
is
Our Salvation!

www.ingramcontent.com/pod-product-compliance
Ingram Content Group UK Ltd.
Pitfield, Milton Keynes, MK11 3LW, UK
UKHW041918190726
13854UKWH00003B/1309

9 781847 280527